Welcome to Our World

SERIES EDITORS
Joan Kang Shin & JoAnn (Jodi) Crandall

AUTHORS
Jill Korey O'Sullivan & Joan Kang Shin

Unit 0 Let's Share! **2**

Unit 1 Stand Up, Sit Down **6**

Unit 2 It's Raining **14**

Unit 3 Wild Animals **22**

Unit 4 Singing and Dancing **30**

Unit 5 See, Smell, Hear **38**

Unit 6 Story Time **46**

Unit 7 It's a Party! **54**

Unit 8 Our World **62**

Projects **70**

The Alphabet **78**

I Can **80**

Puppets

Stickers

NATIONAL GEOGRAPHIC LEARNING | CENGAGE Learning

Australia • Brazil • Japan • Korea • Mexico • Singapore • Spain • United Kingdom • United States

Let's Share!

I need the paint.

I need the paint, too!

Look and listen. TR: 10–11

2

Look and listen. TR: 12–13

1 Stand Up, Sit Down

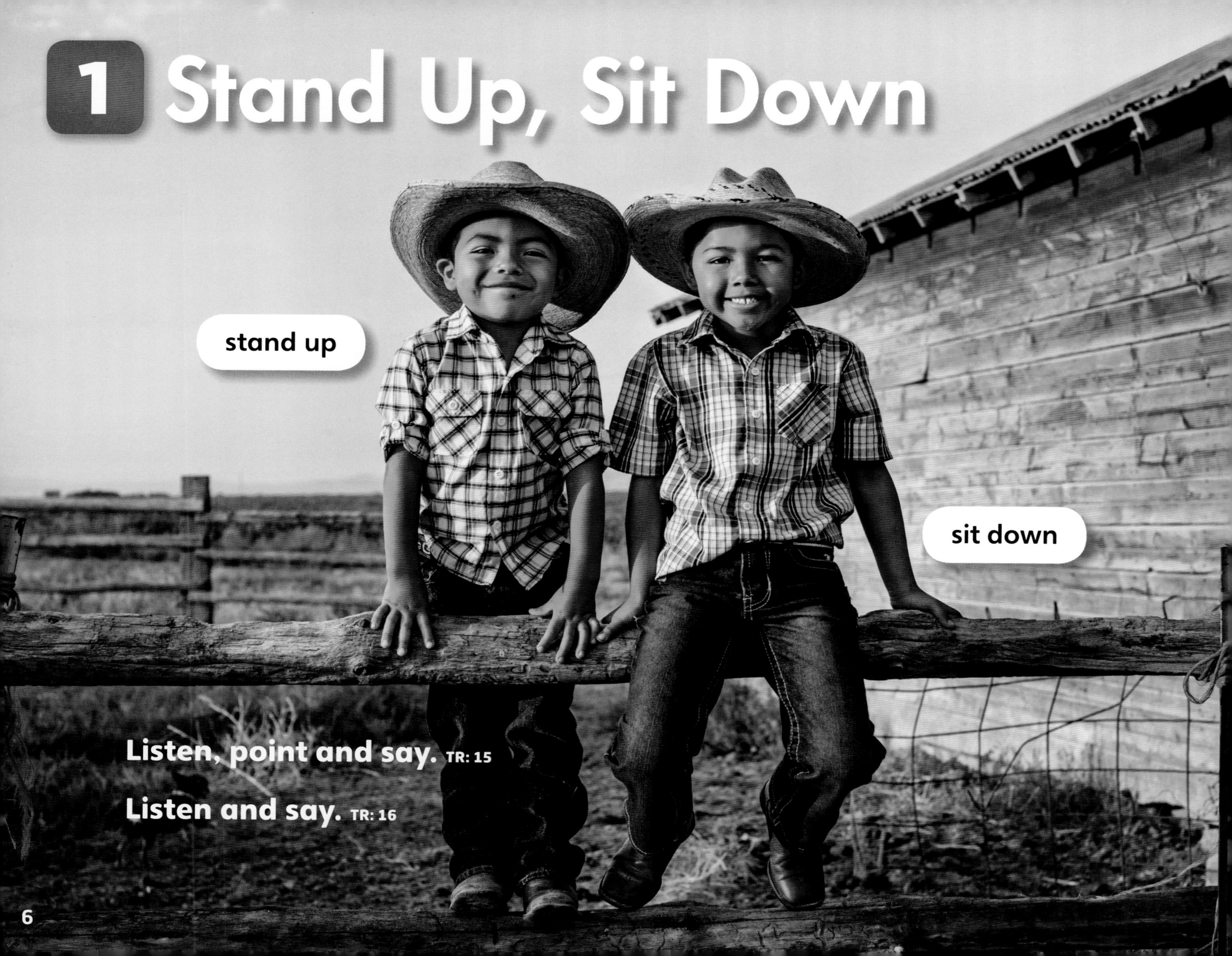

stand up

sit down

Listen, point and say. TR: 15

Listen and say. TR: 16

touch

read

count

write

draw

colour

Look and circle.

Sing. TR: 18

Listen and say. TR: 19

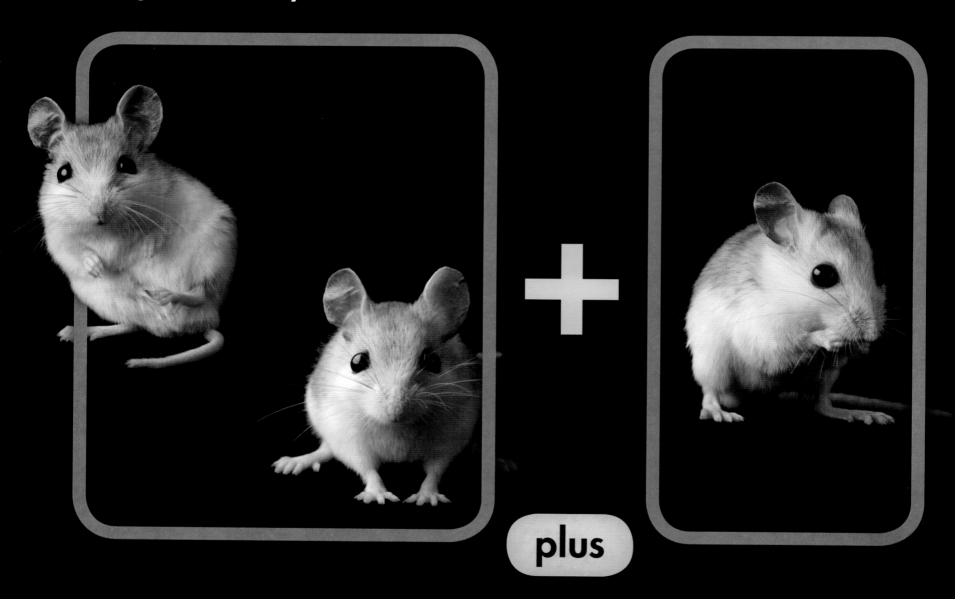

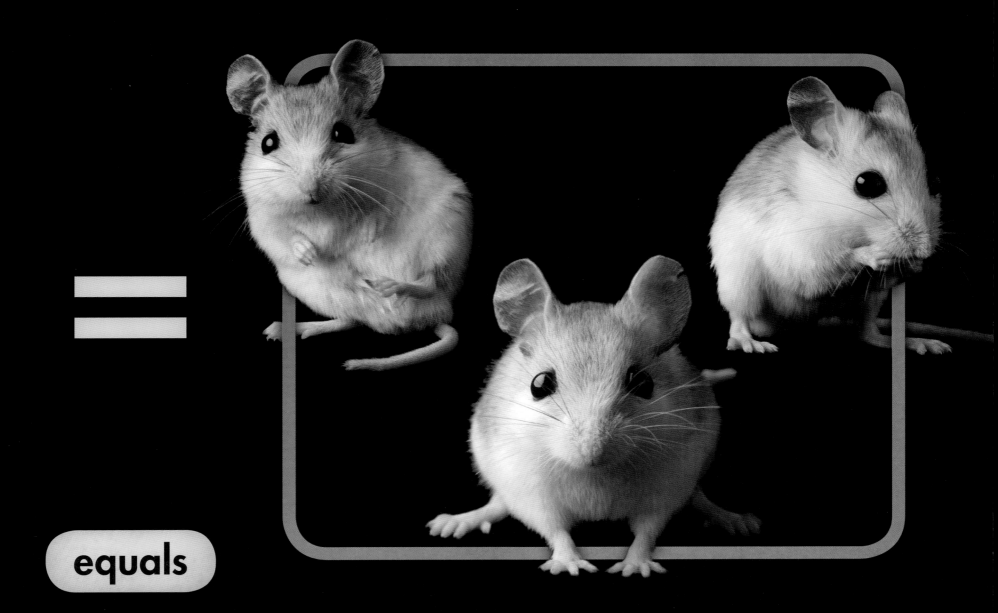

= **equals**

Say and stick.

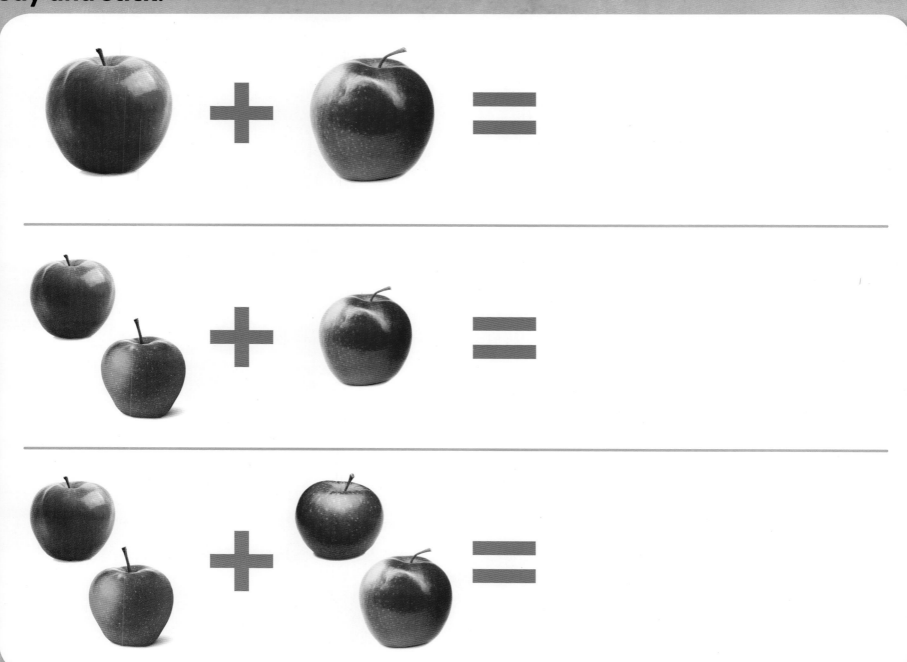

Look and circle.

Listen and say. TR: 21

What do you like doing?

I like drawing.

2 It's Raining

Listen, point and say. TR: 22

Listen and say. TR: 23

raining

windy

cloudy

sunny

snowing

Look and draw a line.

wet

Listen, point and say. TR: 27

dry

Say and stick.

What's the weather like? Colour.

Listen and say. TR: 28

What's the weather like?

It's windy!

3 Wild Animals

Listen, point and say. TR: 29

Listen and say. TR: 30

a monkey

a penguin

a zebra

a lion

an elephant

a tiger

a frog

a panda

Look and draw a line.

Sing. TR: 32

Listen and say. TR: 33

Listen, point and say. TR: 34

big

Say and stick.

What's your favourite animal? Colour.

Listen and say. TR: 35

What's your favourite animal?

An elephant!

Listen, point and say. TR: 36

Listen and say. TR: 37

Listen, point and say. TR: 38–39

Listen and say. TR: 40

singing

clapping

stamping

a drum

a guitar

dancing

shouting

a piano

Draw.

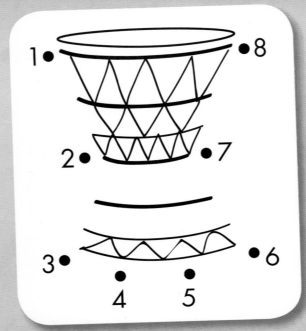

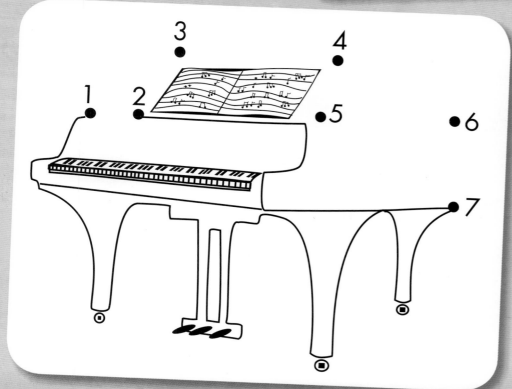

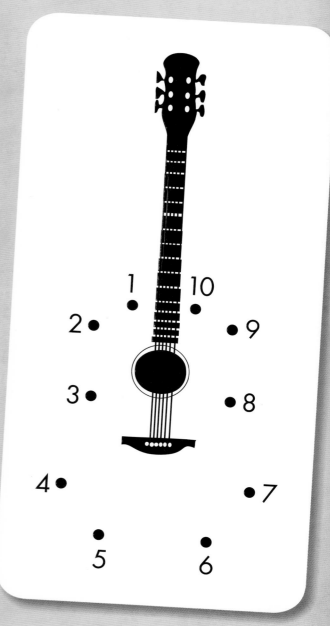

Sing. TR: 41

Listen and say. TR: 42

loud

Listen, point and say. TR: 43

quiet

Say and stick.

Play the game.

What are you doing?

I'm dancing!

5 See, Smell, Hear

Listen, point and say. TR: 45

Listen and say. TR: 46

Listen, point and say. TR: 47

eat

drink

see

smell

feel

hear

taste

Look and circle.

Sing. TR: 48

Listen and say. TR: 49

hard

soft

Say and stick.

Look and circle.
Listen and say. TR: 51

What can you see?

I can see a crayon.

6 Story Time

Listen, point and say. TR: 52

Listen and say. TR: 53

a castle

Listen, point and say. TR: 54

a king

a queen

a princess

a knight

a dragon

a giant

treasure

Look and colour.

     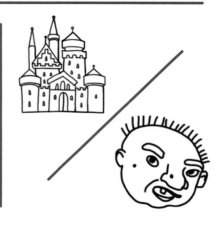

beginning

middle

end

Say and stick.

Stick.

Listen and say. TR: 58

What's the story about?

It's about a king and a dragon.

7 It's a Party!

Listen, point and say. TR: 59

Listen and say. TR: 60

candles

a cake

ice cream

a balloon

pizza

a present

sweets

Look and circle.

Sing. TR: 62

Listen and say. TR: 63

more

Listen, point and say. TR: 64

less

Look and circle *more*.

Stick.

Listen and say. TR: 65

Would you like some ice cream?

Yes, please.

No, thanks.

8 Our World

Listen, point and say. TR: 66

Listen and say. TR: 67

a cloud

a mountain

a bridge

the sky

the sea

a river

a road

Draw.

Sing. TR: 69

Listen and say. TR: 70

the world

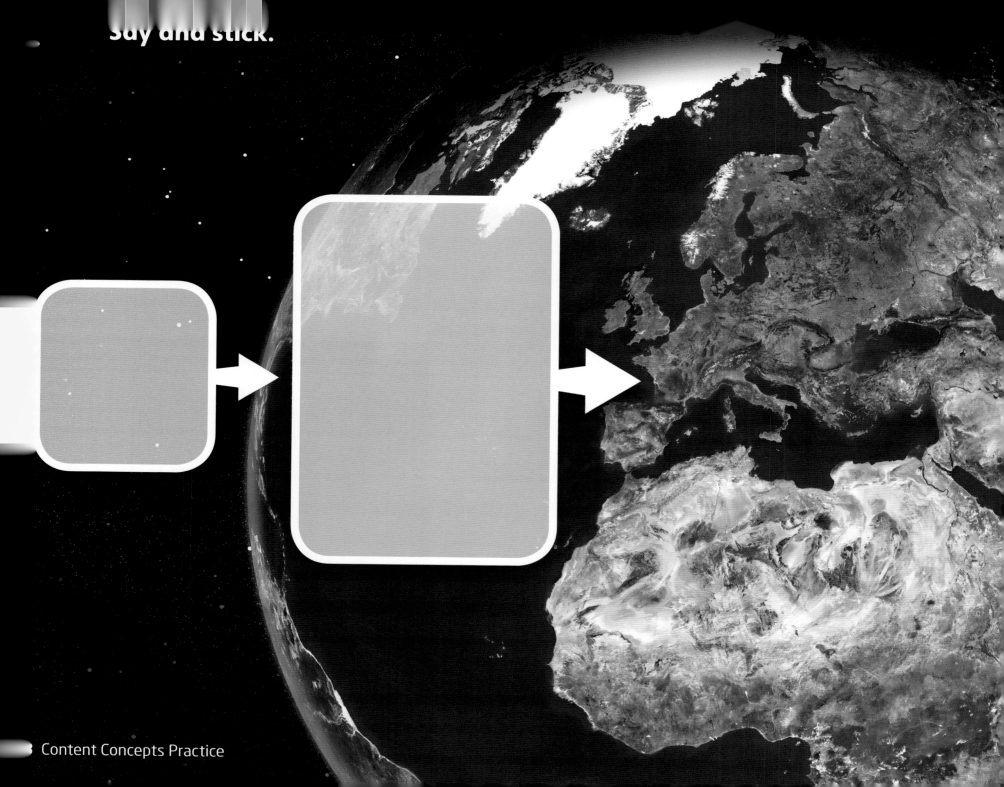

Where do you live?

I live in Spain.

1 Make a counting spider.

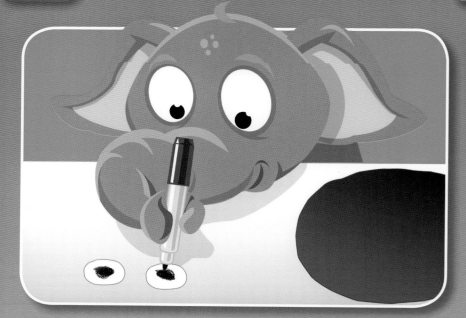

2 Make a rainy day scene.

3 Make a penguin.

4 Make a drum.

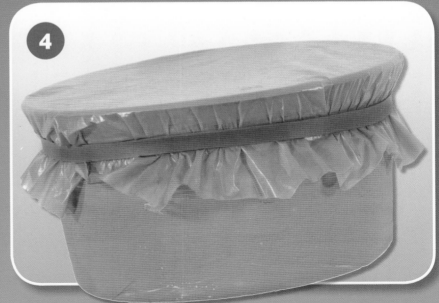

5 Make a five senses poster.

6 Make a dragon.

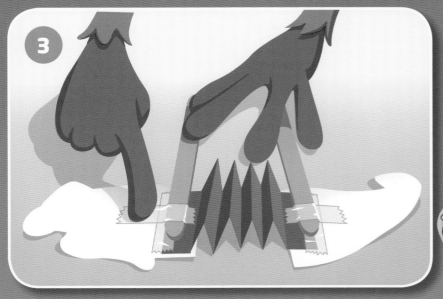

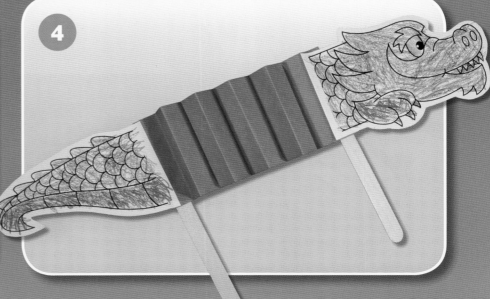

7 Make a pizza.

8 Make a globe.

A apple

B ball

C cat

D dog

E egg

J juice

K king

L lion

M milk

N nose

S socks

T train

U umbrella

V violin

 F   fire engine

 G   goat

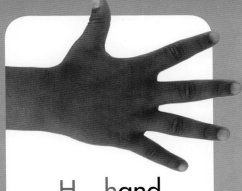 H   hand

 I   igloo

 O   orange

 P   pencil

 Q   queen

 R   rabbit

 W   window

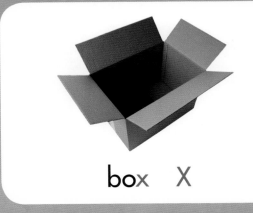 box   X

 Y   yoghurt

 Z   zebra

1 I can talk about my classroom.

2 I can talk about the weather.

3 I can talk about wild animals.

4 I can talk about music.

5 I can talk about feelings.

6 I can talk about stories.

7 I can talk about parties.

8 I can talk about my world.

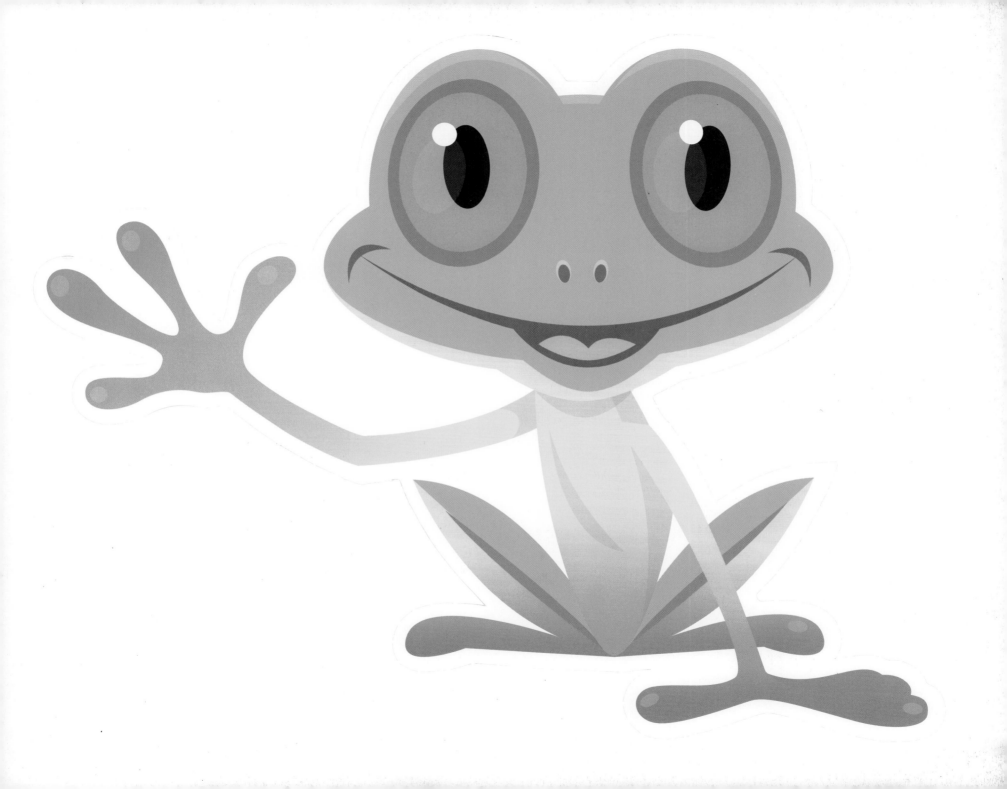

2 It's Raining Stickers

WOW I Can!

1 Stand Up, Sit Down Stickers

WOW I Can!

4 **Singing and Dancing** Stickers

WOW
I Can!

3 **Wild Animals** Stickers

I Can!

6 **Story Time** Stickers

1 2 3

WOW I Can!

5 **See, Smell, Hear** Stickers

WOW I Can!

8 **Our World** Stickers

WOW
I Can!

 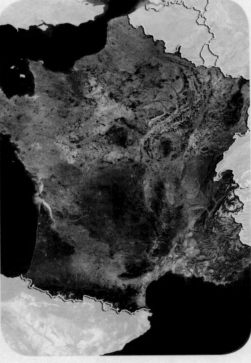

7 **It's a Party!** Stickers

WOW
I Can!